Another "Portals to Personal Power" book by

# TAROT for Beginners
## An Easy-to-Use Beginner's Guide

## Aingeal Rose O'Grady

# Acknowledgements

I wish to thank my beloved husband, the great AHONU (Kevin O'Grady) for being such a wonderful source of inspiration in my life. His encouragement, love, and support have been unending throughout the publication of this book and all my books. We hope his patience, diligence and commitment to excellence have made this Beginner Guide as fun to read and use as it was to put it all together. THANKS AHONU!

This Book uses The Rider Waite Tarot Deck © Published by US Games Inc and created by Arthur Edward Waite.

# Table of Contents

Acknowledgements ................................................................. 3

Introduction ................................................................................7

FAQ about the TAROT ............................................... 8

THE MAJOR ARCANA ............................................... 11

    0 - THE FOOL ................................................................ 11
    1 - THE MAGICIAN ......................................................12
    2 - THE HIGH PRIESTESS ........................................12
    3 - THE EMPRESS ......................................................13
    4 - THE EMPEROR ....................................................14
    5 - THE HIEROPHANT................................................14
    6 - THE LOVERS ........................................................15
    7 - THE CHARIOT ....................................................15
    8 - STRENGTH ..........................................................16
    9 - THE HERMIT ......................................................16
    10 - THE WHEEL OF FORTUNE ............................17
    11 - JUSTICE..............................................................17
    12 - THE HANGED MAN ..........................................18
    13 - DEATH................................................................18
    14 - TEMPERANCE ..................................................19
    15 - THE DEVIL ........................................................19
    16 - THE TOWER ......................................................20
    17 - THE STAR..........................................................20
    18 - THE MOON ........................................................21
    19 - THE SUN ............................................................21
    20 - JUDGMENT ......................................................22
    21 - THE WORLD ....................................................22
THE MINOR ARCANA ............................................... 23

    The 4 Suits ............................................................ 24
        WANDS ............................................................ 25
        CUPS ................................................................ 25
        SWORDS............................................................ 26
        PENTACLES .................................................... 26
    The COURT CARDS ..............................................27
        PAGES................................................................27
        KNIGHTS..........................................................27
        QUEENS ..........................................................27
        KINGS..............................................................27
    THE WANDS ........................................................ 29
        Ace of Wands .................................................. 29
        2 of Wands ...................................................... 29
        3 of Wands ...................................................... 29
        4 of Wands ...................................................... 29

5 of Wands ........................................................................30
6 of Wands ........................................................................30
7 of Wands ........................................................................30
8 of Wands ........................................................................30
9 of Wands ........................................................................31
10 of Wands ......................................................................31
Page of Wands ..................................................................31
Knight of Wands ..............................................................31
Queen of Wands ...............................................................32
King of Wands ..................................................................32
The CUPS ...........................................................................33
Ace of Cups .......................................................................33
2 of Cups ...........................................................................33
3 of Cups ...........................................................................33
4 of Cups ...........................................................................33
5 of Cups ...........................................................................34
6 of Cups ...........................................................................34
7 of Cups ...........................................................................34
8 of Cups ...........................................................................35
9 of Cups ...........................................................................35
10 of Cups .........................................................................35
Page of Cups .....................................................................35
Knight of Cups ..................................................................36
Queen of Cups...................................................................36
King of Cups .....................................................................36
The SWORDS ......................................................................37
Ace of Swords ...................................................................37
2 of Swords .......................................................................37
3 of Swords .......................................................................37
4 of Swords .......................................................................38
5 of Swords .......................................................................38
6 of Swords .......................................................................38
7 of Swords .......................................................................38
8 of Swords .......................................................................39
9 of Swords .......................................................................39
10 of Swords......................................................................39
Page of Swords..................................................................39
Knight of Swords ..............................................................40
Queen of Swords...............................................................40
King of Swords..................................................................40
The PENTACLES..................................................................41
Ace of Pentacles ...............................................................41
2 of Pentacles ...................................................................41
3 of Pentacles ...................................................................41
4 of Pentacles ...................................................................42
5 of Pentacles ...................................................................42

Page | 5

6 of Pentacles ........................................................................ 42
7 of Pentacles ........................................................................ 43
8 of Pentacles ........................................................................ 43
9 of Pentacles ........................................................................ 43
10 of Pentacles ...................................................................... 44
Page of Pentacles................................................................... 44
Knight of Pentacles ............................................................... 44
Queen of Pentacles................................................................ 45
King of Pentacles................................................................... 45
NUMBER VALUES................................................................... 46
ONES..................................................................................... 46
TWOS ................................................................................... 46
THREES ................................................................................ 46
FOURS .................................................................................. 46
FIVES .................................................................................... 46
SIXES .................................................................................... 46
SEVENS ................................................................................ 46
EIGHTS................................................................................. 46
NINES ................................................................................... 46
TENS ..................................................................................... 46
TAROT CARD SPREADS ............................................................47

SIMPLE 3-CARD SPREAD....................................................... 48
Example 3-Card Spread Reading........................................... 48
THE TRADITIONAL CELTIC CROSS SPREAD ...................... 50
Example Celtic Cross Spread Reading ................................... 52
THE MANIFESTATION SPREAD..............................................55
Example Manifesting Spread Reading....................................57
THE PHYSICAL HEALTH SPREAD ........................................ 60
Example Physical Health Spread Reading.............................. 62
INTUITIVE EXERCISE WITH COLOR, NUMBER & SYMBOL.......... 64
Example using the Simple 3 Card Spread............................... 65
MEDITATION WITH THE MAJOR ARCANA............................ 68
Example Meditation with the Major Arcana .......................... 69
About Aingeal Rose ...................................................................72

Page | 6

# Introduction

The TAROT deck has 78 cards in all. These are divided into 22 MAJOR ARCANA and 56 MINOR ARCANA. The history of the TAROT is undetermined but many believe it was created to be a symbolic language to pass down historical and spiritual information at a time when the churches were beginning to censor and persecute those who would not accept their teachings.

The TAROT holds a wealth of historical, alchemical and spiritual information. Meditating on the individual cards in the MAJOR ARCANA for example, can be a journey into advanced states of consciousness. The TAROT is designed to be a spiritual path in its own right, or simply a tool for divination purposes. The TAROT can point out areas in your life that need attention such as lessons you might need to address or to help you understand events and relationships in your life. Moreover, it is an excellent tool to help clarify choices and direction.

In this Easy-to-Use Beginners Guide, you will learn how to read the cards and gain a sustainable foundation for appreciating the deeper aspects of the TAROT. The more you use the cards, the more your intuitive abilities will strengthen.

**HAPPY LEARNING!**

*Aingeal Rose O'Grady*

# FAQ about the TAROT

### Q.   How do I pick a deck?

**A.**   The Rider-Waite deck is the most frequently used deck for beginners because its symbolism is the easiest and most clear to read; however, I recommend picking a deck that "talks" to you when you look at the pictures. This means that you start to feel things or receive impressions or ideas as soon as you look at the images on the cards. The reason this is desirable is because the TAROT is designed to stimulate the connection between your intuitive self and your conscious mind. You want to choose a deck that provides this for you.

### Q.   How do I treat my deck?

**A.**   I always keep my cards in a wooden box or cloth bag. Some people like to wrap their cards in silk or satin. The common theme here is to keep them covered when not in use - this is because the cards emit vibrations and also absorb energies from the environment they are in. You want to keep your deck as clear and clean as possible when you are doing a reading.

### Q.   How do I clear my deck?

**A.**   You can clear a TAROT deck simply by shuffling them with the focused intention to clear them. Other ways are to spread them out in a quiet room in the sunlight for a few hours or burn some sage around them. Some people like to diffuse a high frequency essential oil near them, such as jasmine, sandalwood, frankincense or ylang ylang. Another way is to hold them to your heart and send love into them.

### Q.   What is a 'querent'?

**A.**   A 'querent' is the person who the reading is for i.e. the one who is asking the question in the reading. Of course that can be yourself if it is you that needs the answers.

### Q.   How many times do I shuffle the cards for a reading?

**A.**   As many times as you want! You will feel when you have shuffled enough - it may be a few times or many times. Trust yourself with this - there is no right or wrong way to do it.

*Q.     When I am doing a reading for a client, should I shuffle the cards for them or let them shuffle?*

*A.*     You can do it either way. I like to let my clients shuffle while they are focusing on their concerns because I believe you get a more accurate reading if your client's energy goes into the cards. However, there are readers who prefer to be the one shuffling for their client. It is strictly up to you which way you want to do it.

As you progress, you may want to have several decks, each for different purposes. I use three decks for example; I have one that is just to read clients, one for my own personal use and one for teaching.

*Q.     How do I pull the cards from the deck?*

*A.*     You can pull cards from anywhere in the deck. Some people pull all their cards from the top, some pull from the middle and others pull from random places in the deck. All are fine to do.

*Q.     Do I pull the cards all upright or upright and reversed?*

*A.*     You can do it either way, but whichever way you choose, give that message to your subconscious mind **before** you begin shuffling. You will then have an accurate reading either way.

*Q.     I have a hard time getting the meaning from all the cards - how do they all go together?*

*A.*     It is important to keep in mind the (1) **POSITION** of the cards and what that position is (2) **REPRESENTING.** Also keep in mind your clients (3) **QUESTIONS** as you are examining the cards. If you do these 3 things you will see that a spread becomes like a story and each position builds on the one behind it, like steps. There are times however, when the cards do not seem to answer your clients' question - in these cases, see what the spread **IS** addressing and go from there. Sometimes a person's Higher Self has something more important to address first.

Also practice the exercise in this book entitled **INTUITIVE EXERCISE WITH COLOR, NUMBER & SYMBOL.** This exercise will develop your intuition to where you will not even need to remember the cards 'official' meanings.

**Q.    Aren't all reversed cards negative?**

**A.**    No, some cards are better in their reversed positions. You have a choice when using the TAROT and doing a spread to pull the cards either solely UPRIGHT or UPRIGHT & REVERSED.  Many users of the TAROT like to let the cards fall as they may while other users prefer to turn all the cards UPRIGHT.  I have personally done it both ways, but now I pull them all upright. There is no right way or wrong way to do it. What I DO suggest, however, is to decide ahead of time which way you are going to lay your spread out. This will give the message to your subconscious mind and will assure you of an accurate answer to your query or focus.

To accommodate both schools of thought, I have provided in this book both upright and reversed aspects of each card, giving you the option to intuit meanings from both.

**Q.    Are TAROT cards evil?**

**A.**    The TAROT is a tool for self discovery, and this is not to underestimate their powerful symbolism. They were branded evil by the power structures of the churches to have people turn their power over to the church authorities. USED CORRECTLY, the TAROT will bring forth enlightenment, refinement of character and wisdom. However, do not use the TAROT to invade someone else's privacy - that is a misuse of it!

**Q.    Is it important to psychically protect myself while reading the cards?**

**A.**    Yes, it is crucial to protect yourself at all times, not only while you are doing a reading. We are living in fast-changing times and people's attitudes about the TAROT simply reflect that huge shift in the growth of awareness around psychic development. I mean it is both very good and getting progressively very bad.

Looking back over my 35 years of Metaphysical teaching and consciously staying at the cutting edge of Psychic and Spiritual developments, I have found the best protection is the **Maharic Shield**.

You can find it on the **Azurite Press** website at http://azuritepress.com - search for **Maharic Shield**. I encourage you to practice this protection every day, but especially when you engage with a client for a reading.

**Happy learning and remember, practice makes perfect!**

# THE MAJOR ARCANA

The Major Cards are numbered from 0 to 21. They indicate stages of personal development, personality and character refinement, virtues, lessons, realizations, warnings, advice, historical information, energy moving beneath everyday situations, alchemical forces at work, spiritual development, inter-dimensional information, and cosmic cycles.

In this section, I list all the cards in ascending numeric order. For each one, I explain the meaning of the card at the **Mundane** level and the **Spiritual** level. I list out the **Lessons** of each card, the **Misuse** of the energy of the card and finally, I explain the meaning of the **Number** itself in the context of the card.

## 0 - THE FOOL

**MUNDANE** - New beginnings, starting out on a journey, taking risks, innocence or naiveté, new adventures, freedom, purity, protection, idealism, trust, simplicity, a carefree attitude.

**SPIRITUAL** - Beginning or completing a spiritual journey, merkaba science, union with all, perfection, super-consciousness, spiritual purity, rising above duality to union.

**LESSON** - Being at a crossroads where the choice that is made is very important as to the future direction, learning to trust one's spiritual life, the purification of one's intentions and desires.

**MISUSE** - Foolish behavior, immaturity, look before you leap, watch where you are going, taking unnecessary risks, a need to be more careful in one's decisions and behaviors, recklessness.

**NUMBER** - Zero is the beginning and the end where all things originate and to where they return to union.

# 1 - THE MAGICIAN

**MUNDANE** - The conscious mind, independence, willpower, focused attention, deliberate action, choice, decisions, personal power, concentration, right direction.

**SPIRITUAL** - Principle of 'as above so below', or 'like attracts like', becoming a conscious creator, using the forces of nature to manifest responsibly and for the good of all. Using your will to effect positive growth and change in your life or environment.

**LESSON** - Taking responsibility for one's life and decisions, focusing attention to achieve a goal, using power wisely, respecting all life and free will choice, using your mind and heart or 'will and passion' to promote life and positive creativity, honoring and respecting the natural world.

THE MAGICIAN.

**MISUSE** - Using your will or personal power over others, using manifesting for selfish purposes that manipulate others, using the forces of nature for spells, curses etc.

**NUMBER** - The number 1 can mean the beginning of something, new energy or inspiration, initial stages or taking the initiative to begin or to change, an onrush of energy that is available for use.

# 2 - THE HIGH PRIESTESS

**MUNDANE** - Femininity, secrets, virgins or virginity, barren, non-activity, passivity, truth not revealed, wait before you act, things germinating but not yet in form, having faith in your own feelings, look deeper or beneath the surface of things, fertility problems.

**SPIRITUAL** - The subconscious mind, esoteric information, deep intuition or psychic abilities developed or developing, secret societies, the feminine principle as a source of creative power, feminine goddesses such as the Virgin Mary, Isis, Quan Yin, Shakti, Aphrodite, Danu and Pele to name a few.

THE HIGH PRIESTESS

**LESSON** - Learning to get close to your own feelings, trusting your intuition, learning about your feminine power and using it in a balanced way, learning about the subconscious mind and how to direct it, researching esoteric knowledge.

**MISUSE** -  Remaining too passive, or forcing something into being which needs time to unfold, using feminine power to dominate or manipulate, remaining quiet or not following your intuition when you know you should, timidity, keeping secrets that should be revealed.

**NUMBER** - The number 2 indicates duality, positive and negative forces as part of creation, inner and outer, feminine vs. masculine, light vs. dark, wisdom vs. ignorance etc.

# 3 - THE EMPRESS

**MUNDANE** - Fertility, pregnancy, mothers or motherhood, love, things coming to fruition, nurturing,   home, beauty, lush environment, growth, prosperity, having needs fulfilled, all is good, rewards are near.

**SPIRITUAL** - Nature, the Divine Mother/Goddess, Mother Earth, the influence of Venus, woman as a creative force, love as the driving force beneath all creation.

**LESSON** - The correct use of nurturing and mothering, unresolved mother issues, abundance, giving and receiving, acceptance.

**MISUSE** - Over-mothering, over-bearing, over-nurturing, irresponsible pregnancy, giving too much, need to learn to receive, denying oneself at the expense of others, shame which is causing self-reproach, not pregnant.

**NUMBER** - The number 3 signifies things coming together, success, culmination, fertility, abundance, celebration.

# 4 - THE EMPEROR

**MUNDANE** - Father or fatherhood, boss, structure, discipline, order, routine, ego, ruler, dominance, material world, control, power, balance and authority over your own world, respect.

**SPIRITUAL** - Divine Order, Spiritual Ruler, dominion over Earthly matters, correct use of Power, Self Authority.

**LESSON** - The correct use of power, using the ego in service to the Higher Self as opposed to the Lower self, being a force for good rather than the ego, overcoming abusive patterns, being able to see other points of view.

**MISUSE** - Abuse of power or force, domination, possessiveness, rigidity, over-inflated ego, dogmatic, set-in-ways, abusive father, boss, religious person, or other authority figure, using anger to bully others.

**NUMBER** - The number 4 is solid, stable, rigid, set, has form, order, structure, discipline, and is responsible and secure.

# 5 - THE HIEROPHANT

**MUNDANE** - Church, traditions, marriage, religion, dogma, belief systems, stubbornness, outside appearance is important.

**SPIRITUAL** - Higher Self, Adept, higher guide, esoteric knowledge, meditation, priesthood, ministry, going within, Divine Truth.

**LESSON** - Turning within for Truth, allowing others to have their faith and beliefs without judgment, respecting tradition while being able to become reliant on your own Inner Self.

**MISUSE** - Stuck in old belief structures or dogmas, too preachy, controlling others through religion, tradition or dogma, relying on outside authorities rather than going within to your own internal guidance.

**NUMBER** - The number 5 is a catalyst to higher growth, change and movement.

# 6 - THE LOVERS

**MUNDANE** - Relationships, lovers, sexuality, choices, male and female issues, romance, unions, love affairs, sacred versus profane love, two paths, choose with integrity, seek spiritual values carefully.

**SPIRITUAL** - Sacred union of male and female, Divine Love, Divine relationships. Sacred sex, inner marriage of male and female aspects within oneself, anima, animus.

**LESSON** - All relationship issues, respecting men and women/male and female principles, equality, commitment, using sex appropriately, loyalty, discrimination.

**MISUSE** - Being unfaithful, using sex inappropriately, focusing only on bodily pleasures, disrespecting men or women, not honoring the equality of the masculine and feminine principles in creation and within oneself.

**NUMBER** - The number 6 has to do with balance, victory, home, family, success and harmony.

# 7 - THE CHARIOT

**MUNDANE** - Movement, journey, travel, physical health, car issues, decisions, self control, tension between two different directions, self-discipline, honor or reward is due, victory, self esteem, healthy ego and personality, behaving responsibly.

**SPIRITUAL** - The Merkaba Vehicle, the Divine Chariot, wheels-within-wheels, the light and dark within oneself, wisdom.

**LESSON** - Balancing the light and dark within the personality, self control, respect of the body as a temple and vehicle, patience, letting go of the past.

**MISUSE** - Selfishness, playing both sides of a situation for personal gain, health issues, not moving forward by not making a decision, self control issues, lack of self esteem, recklessness in any area of life.

**NUMBER** - The number 7 is about victory, success, spiritual awareness beginning, divine help and inspiration, a degree of enlightenment, challenges overcome.

# 8 - STRENGTH

**MUNDANE** - Strength, perseverance, healing, getting the help you need, comfort, subduing egoist tendencies, assurance, peace, nurturing, use love, patience and gentleness, remove blocks.

**SPIRITUAL** - Faith, patience, love over fear, kindness, Divine comfort, strength and protection, purification of the instinctual self.

**LESSON** - Acknowledging the instinctual nature but not allowing it to run your life, love vs. ego, use gentleness not force or aggression, kindness rather than judgment, having the ego/instinctual/animal nature in service to the heart.

**MISUSE** - Cruelty, ego domination, selfishness, heartlessness, weakness, giving up, allowing the body's desires to run the show, impatience, judgment.

**NUMBER** - The number 8 has to do with power, executive force, success and expertise.

# 9 - THE HERMIT

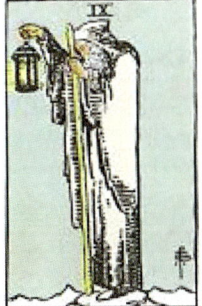

**MUNDANE** - Self reflection, inner contemplation, aloneness, retreat or retreat centers, healing, isolation, hermit. May show depression.

**SPIRITUAL** - Enlightenment, guide or teacher for others, monk, sage, 'Ask and you shall receive', 'Knock and the door will open', Divine Counsel or counselor, seeker of Truth, healer.

**LESSON** - Balancing healthy retreat with withdrawal, service to others, patience, experiment carefully, finding answers within.

**MISUSE** - Self imposed loneliness, too reclusive, not letting your light shine, withdrawing from society, inability or refusal to serve others, suicidal tendencies, self pity.

**NUMBER** - The number 9 concerns culminations, peaks, conclusions, endings, fulfillments, and gestation periods.

# 10 - THE WHEEL OF FORTUNE

**MUNDANE** - Change, movement, cycles, good or bad luck, new information coming in, the wheels of fate are turning, rotation, ups and downs, look up when down, adapt to change, look at new ideas.

**SPIRITUAL** - Cosmic cycles, destinies, divine knowledge, change as a constant, world events.

**LESSON** - Understanding and accepting change as part of life, timing, how cycles affect us, flowing with ups and downs, mastering your destiny.

**MISUSE** - Refusal to accept change, allowing fate only to determine your destiny, resistance to growth and forward movement.

**NUMBER** - The number 10 is accumulation, conclusion, attainment, increase (either positive or negative), new beginnings after a cycle.


# 11 - JUSTICE

**MUNDANE** -Fair decisions, balanced judgment, court cases or issues with the law, balance, what you sow you will reap, judges, lawyers, lesson learned, right decision.

**SPIRITUAL** - Karmic debts, past life issues, the Law of Cause & Effect.

**LESSON** - Balancing judgment with mercy, honesty, decisions, balancing karma, fairness.

**MISUSE** - Judging others, decision not favorable, merciless, blaming others, lack of forgiveness, unbalanced in some way, things not reconciled, unfairness to others.

**NUMBER** - The number 11 is about duality, denotes issues are of spiritual importance, balance, proportion, weighing sides, decisions important, two ways of looking at something.

# 12 - THE HANGED MAN

**MUNDANE** - Feeling of or being hung up temporarily, new decisions, stagnation in a situation, timing not right, need to wait.

**SPIRITUAL** - Surrendering to your higher will, lifting the veil to a higher sight, the martyr.

**LESSON** - Selfless service, enlightenment gained by reversing the way you see the world, balancing sacrifice with self love.

**MISUSE** - Refusal to see something differently, martyr complex, stubbornness which causes stagnation or lack of progress or growth, playing the victim for selfish purposes.

**NUMBER** - The number 12 is about gearing up to a change that has much potential for growth, getting ready, preparing the way, and laying the groundwork for a new opportunity or path.

# 13 - DEATH

**MUNDANE** - Making a sudden change, new life entirely, no going back, moving forward despite obstacles. It can indicate physical death in RARE instances.

**SPIRITUAL** - Release of old belief systems and ways of doing things, inner and outer purification, shifting from outward authorities to your own Inner Authority.

**LESSON** - Letting go of the past, ability to flow with major change, transforming, strength to accept a new life.

**MISUSE** - Refusing to move forward or change, resistance to what is happening in one's life, letting outer influences tell you what to do and ignoring your own inner urges to grow and move forward.

**NUMBER** - The number 13 is about a pivotal moment or time pointing to major turning points in one's life. These moments can be life changing and indicate periods of tremendous growth and opportunity.

# 14 - TEMPERANCE

**MUNDANE** - Blending, balancing extremes, trying new ideas and things but keeping security, maintain balance while you plan, don't overdo it, consider carefully what is needed to achieve your goal and take the appropriate steps. Be patient and look at all aspects. You have Divine Guidance.

**SPIRITUAL** - Twin Flame relationships, inner alchemy, androgyny, union of opposites, Higher Self, Guardian Angel.

**LESSON** - Tempering aspects of oneself to achieve a high goal, moderation, not going to extremes, keeping your inner calm and observing carefully before taking action.

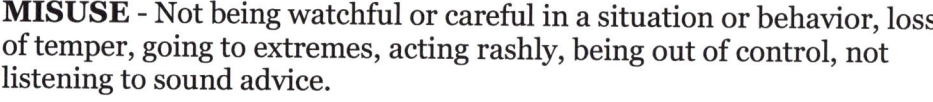

**MISUSE** - Not being watchful or careful in a situation or behavior, loss of temper, going to extremes, acting rashly, being out of control, not listening to sound advice.

**NUMBER** - The number 14 has to do with coming to a state of equilibrium after a major change, a period of great accomplishment and/or opportunity.

# 15 - THE DEVIL

**MUNDANE** - Temptations, limitations, submission, fears, self imposed restrictions, possible nervous breakdown, repressed energies, inhibitions, negative energies influencing someone's life or a situation in life.

**SPIRITUAL** - Pan, honoring the power in nature, the right use of ritual and power for the good of all.

**LESSON** - Overcoming deep seated fears which limit or repress, freeing oneself from self imposed restrictions or situations, overcoming abuse, the realization that we imprison ourselves by our own beliefs and fears, taking back our personal power.

**MISUSE** - Black magic, perverted sexuality, lack of conscious or heart, domination over others, curses, spells, too materialistic, abuse in any form, addictions, limiting anyone's freedom, obsession with the body, selfishness, possessions.

**NUMBER** - 15 is a precarious number in that it can bring forth odd events and circumstance. It is a time to be watchful and more self aware, examining motives and the motives of others. It is an opening number and where it will lead depends upon the mindfulness of those involved.

# 16 - THE TOWER

**MUNDANE** - Upheavals which shake up existing comfort zones causing change, shaking the foundations, lightning strikes, earthquakes, accidents, a wake-up call, an influx of electrical frequency causing or forcing change for positive or negative, rapid change, breakdown of permanent situations.

**SPIRITUAL** - Sudden awakening, ego purification, cosmic events, earth changes.

**LESSON** - Keep growing and flow with the change as refusal to do so will cause a buildup of resistance which will inevitably lead to destruction or upheaval of some kind. You can avoid the turmoil if you flow with the needed change.

**MISUSE** - Ignoring signs which warn of trouble or health problems if action isn't taken for improvement.

**NUMBER** - The number 16 indicates an accumulation or buildup of energy which is coming to a head for positive or negative depending on how it is used or dispersed.

# 17 - THE STAR

**MUNDANE** - Positive turn of events, healing of self, physical wellbeing, individuality, blending of opposites, nothing to hide, health, hope, promise, positive future, appreciating and nourishing the land and the environment.

**SPIRITUAL** - Cosmic blessings, 'star' energy which heals, spiritual guidance and protection, Divine inspiration.

**LESSON** - Self honesty which leads to self healing, being comfortable with your body, balancing the emotions with physical life, taking care of your health.

**MISUSE** - Not taking care of oneself and body, lack of inspiration, poor health, not recovering as quickly as had hoped, poor self esteem, being out of balance or harmony with the earth, unwilling to be self honest which would promote healing, health, and positive growth.

**NUMBER** - The number 17 has a highly positive energy supportive of health, healing and all things positive. It is a positive influence leading to new growth and renewal and setting the stage for further illumination.

# 18 - THE MOON

**MUNDANE** - Cycles, timing, menstrual cycles, magnetism, hormone fluctuations, magnification of personal issues resulting in an increase of emotional intensity for positive or negative, allow intuition to guide you.

**SPIRITUAL** - Illumination, increase in psychic abilities, higher understanding perhaps of a cosmic nature, the Shadow self.

**LESSON** - Emotional balance, what is real and what is illusion, learning to trust yourself and your intuition, understanding right timing and cosmic fluctuations, heeding warnings when they occur, self reflection.

**MISUSE** - Emotional imbalance/reaction, deception, insanity, danger, disillusionment, ignoring warnings or your own intuition.

**NUMBER** - The number 18 is a number of 'testing' which should strengthen the emotional and psychic bodies. It can indicate a warning to watch these bodies for illusion or deception as energy fluctuations increase and decrease.

# 19 - THE SUN

**MUNDANE** - Freedom, warmth, joy, happiness, excellent for marriage, expansion, uplifting, success, vitality, renewal, openness, freedom of expression, good health, many blessings, growth of wealth and health. This card offsets other cards in the spread that may be negative.

**SPIRITUAL** - The Divine Inner Child, regeneration, healing on every level, the navel and solar plexus chakras as seats for renewal.

**LESSON** - Healing the Inner Child, returning to joy and innocence in full consciousness, being open to receive.

**MISUSE** - Using energy for solely selfish purposes, inhibitions, refusal to grow up, play and work not balanced, ill health, navel and solar plexus chakras in need of attention.

**NUMBER** - 19 is a 'crescendo' number filled with positive potential and protection. It is joyous and supportive of new endeavors with the energy behind it for success.

# 20 - JUDGMENT

**MUNDANE** - Truth revealed in a situation or relationship, honesty, coming alive after a period of illness or stagnation, decisions, awakening or new awareness, being realistic, bouncing back from difficulty, healing on many levels, hearing issues.

**SPIRITUAL** - Resurrection of the body, forgiveness, truth revealed, Divine announcements or declarations, healing with sound, clairaudience.

**LESSON** - Releasing judgments upon self or others, forgiving the past, seeing and accepting Truth, waking up to cosmic or world events, God is Love, death is not real, learning to listen and hear.

**MISUSE** - Judging and not forgiving others, denying Truth, perpetuating fear dogmas, the belief in death, not listening.

**NUMBER** - The number 20 is the number of climax times 2! Key phrases would be - 'This is It', 'Now's the time', 'Seeing is believing', 'Wake up!', 'Hear me!'

# 21 - THE WORLD

**MUNDANE** - Wholeness, completion, fulfillment, perfect balance, equilibrium, success, satisfaction, triumphant in any undertaking.

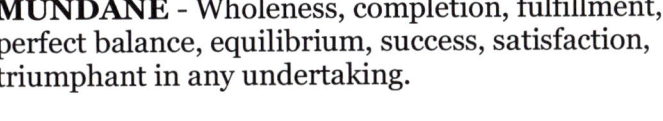

**SPIRITUAL** - Ascension of body or consciousness, transfiguration, triumph, union with the Divine, holding the center point of equilibrium between 2 poles of tension.

**LESSON** - Rising above duality, maintaining balance, self fulfillment and satisfaction in any area of life, achieving union with the cosmos by holding your own inner pillar amidst the chaos of the outer world.

**MISUSE** - Falling out of harmony with the whole, wanting to remain separate, refusal to learn or gain knowledge, lack of personal fulfillment or the fulfillment of a goal.

**NUMBER** - The number 21 indicates the arrival of a certain state of consciousness, a level of attainment, self mastery, and high achievement. From here, an even greater cycle of growth will ensue.

# THE MINOR ARCANA

There are **4 SUITS** in the MINOR ARCANA

1. **Wands**
2. **Cups**
3. **Swords**
4. **Pentacles**.

Each suit represents an **ELEMENT**

1. **Fire**
2. **Water**
3. **Air**
4. **Earth**

Each suit represents a **SEASON** of the year

1. **Spring**
2. **Summer**
3. **Autumn**
4. **Winter**

Each **SUIT** represents **3 ASTROLOGICAL** signs

1. **Wands** - Aries, Leo & Sagittarius
2. **Cups** - Pisces, Cancer & Scorpio
3. **Swords** - Aquarius, Libra & Gemini
4. **Pentacles** - Capricorn, Taurus & Virgo

Each suit is numbered from **1-10** and has 4 Court cards per suit

Court cards are **PEOPLE** cards; **Page, Knight, Queen & King** in each suit.

The MINOR ARCANA will show you how the energies of the MAJOR cards play out in daily life through careers, relationships, thoughts and material accomplishments.

While this may seem complex at first, it very soon becomes second nature to you. On the next page I have laid out a summary chart which makes it easier to see the relationships at a glance.

# The 4 Suits

| SUIT IMAGE | WANDS | CUPS | SWORDS | PENTACLES |
|---|---|---|---|---|
| | ACE of WANDS. | ACE of CUPS. | ACE of SWORDS. | ACE of PENTACLES |
| ELEMENT | Fire | Water | Air | Earth |
| SEASON | Summer | Spring | Autumn | Winter |
| SIGN | Aries | Pisces | Aquarius | Capricorn |
| | Leo | Cancer | Libra | Taurus |
| | Sagittarius | Scorpio | Gemini | Virgo |

## Notes:

# WANDS

**Element**: Fire

**Season**: Summer

**Astrological Signs**: Aries, Leo, Sagittarius

The **WANDS** are a **CREATIVE** suit and deal with things movable. Because it is the **fire** element, it is aggressive, changeable, dynamic, inspirational, powerful, sexual, energizing, overwhelming, outgoing, motivating, electric, intense, unpredictable, and attractive.

The **WANDS** deal with creativity, career, personal power, personal vitality, sexuality, how you extend or express yourself externally.

# CUPS

**Element**: Water

**Season**: Spring

**Astrological Signs**: Pisces, Cancer, Scorpio

The **CUPS** are an **EMOTIONAL** suit and deal with things fluid. Because it is the **water** element it is movable, changeable flowing or stagnant, intuitive, feeling, psychic, knowing, communicative, connecting, reflective, internal, spiritual, and deep.

The **CUPS** deal with relationships, friendships, romances, spirituality, emotions, truth, trust, communication, and all heart-centered issues.

# SWORDS

**Element**: Air

**Season**: Autumn

**Astrological Signs**: Aquarius, Libra, Gemini

The **SWORDS** are an **AIRY** suit and deal with imagination, thoughts, perceptions, opinions, beliefs, power, force, aggression, ideas, intangibility, courage, decisions, life and death. Because it is the **air** element this suit can deal with things not yet in form but mostly in the querents thoughts or perceptions.

The SWORDS are about how you look at the world, what you and others think, believe and perceive - ideas, how choice and decision is used, the use of the mind for positive or negative, and courage or lack of it.

# PENTACLES

**Element**: Earth

**Season**: Winter

**Astrological Signs**: Capricorn, Taurus, Virgo

The **PENTACLES** are an **EARTHY** suit and deal with things solid, set, material, in form, planetary, accomplished, grounded, tangible, external, demonstrated, seen, secure, stable and structured. Because it is the **earth** element, this suit represents things fixed and most likely already in form.

The **PENTACLES** reflect physical earth life and status - business, finances, home, security, materialism, health, personal sense of self value, herbalism, planetary work, well-being and success.

# The COURT CARDS

There are **4 COURT CARDS** per suit. Each represents a person or level of maturity in the suit described.

## PAGES

Pages represent youths from birth to 25 years. They can also be messengers bringing news. They are the most immature or undeveloped in personality and character traits of the suit. As a person they will carry the attributes of the suit they represent.

## KNIGHTS

Knights represent young adults to adults from 25 to 40 years. They usually represent some sort of movement or activity in the suit described and can still be relatively immature or growing. They carry the personality attributes of the suit they represent.

## QUEENS

Queens represent girls or women from 18 years and up. They are fairly mature or matronly. They may be in positions of authority and they carry the personality attributes of the suit they represent.

## KINGS

KINGS represent men from 40 years on up. They are fairly mature or fatherly. They may be in positions of authority or prestige. They carry the personality attributes of the suit they represent.

All **COURT CARDS** can show aspects of maturity or immaturity for people of all ages. For example, you could have an older man or a woman who may turn up as a Page in a certain suit indicating that they have not mastered or matured in an area of their lives corresponding to the traits or elements of that suit.

Conversely, you could have a young person show up as a Queen or King of a particular suit, indicating a level of maturity in the traits of that particular suit.

Practicing with the TAROT will help you become sensitive to the Court cards in this way.

In the next section, we will examine each card in each suit sequentially, providing you with the meaning of each, both upright and reversed.

## Notes:

# THE WANDS

### Ace of Wands

**Upright** - New career opportunity, onrush of creative/inspirational energy, sexual vitality or opportunity, dynamic force, expressing oneself creatively, drive, ambition.

**Reversed** - Energy for change or inspiration is brief and weak, opportunity lost, failure to act when time was ripe.

### 2 of Wands

**Upright** - career or personal partnerships, decisions, choices, options, planetary healing work, travel in or out of the country, joint efforts, common purpose, and connection to certain land areas.

**Reversed** - Partnerships or projects not working out, travel plans delayed or canceled, compromise needed, important decision not being made, neither option satisfactory, missing factors.

### 3 of Wands

**Upright** - Coming together of career opportunities, travel or a trip, movement to a new location, considering new possibilities, job that has you relocate or travel, group effort.

**Reversed** - Time to travel delayed or not right, dreaming of change but not practical at the moment, not the right place or time to move, confused as to what opportunity to choose or which way to go.

### 4 of Wands

**Upright** - Celebration of success, harmonious work or personal life, weddings, stability, fruitfulness, friends, living in harmony with the Earth.

**Reversed** - Home life or marriage not in harmony, career may be falling apart or changing, security being uprooted, cooperation may be lacking.

Page | 29

### 5 of Wands

**Upright** - Building something as a group , teamwork, sports games, sparring,  join forces, cooperative effort, each person's input is valuable.

**Reversed** - Scattered energies or ideas, things not coming together, chaos, quarreling, creative abilities not focused, 'too many chiefs and not enough Indians', no one is cooperating.

### 6 of Wands

**Upright** - Promotion at work or other advancement, success, leadership role, victory in an undertaking, positive cycle, peace is achieved, positive movement, job opportunity in a new location.

**Reversed** - No promotion, position weakened, not using leadership potential or not doing a job properly, walking away from an opportunity, need more confidence in your abilities to succeed or lead, gifts being wasted in favor of security.

### 7 of Wands

**Upright** - Meeting challenges head on, being challenged, defense for good or ill, perseverance, strength to succeed, trying to maintain equilibrium amid opposing forces, may have hands in too many projects at once.

**Reversed** - Feeling weak or unable to defend oneself, not up to the challenge, weariness, obstacles lightening up or leaving, jealousy abated, maintaining a position through sheer determination.

### 8 of Wands

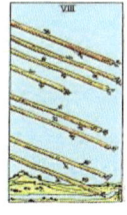

**Upright** - Many opportunities appearing suddenly, travel, moving location, fast-moving energy, sexual advances, trip over land, powerful options, heading east.

**Reversed** - Opportunities, but not as many, slower movement, looking backward instead of forward, may need to go 'home' for a time, look to your past to find yourself.

Page | 30

### 9 of Wands

**Upright** - Caution, hesitation, review before deciding, suspicion, wait, time for recovery and stepping back, look at other options, uncertainty, not sure of who to trust, take time to heal.

**Reversed** - OK to act now, path ahead is open, freedom from strife or toil, things easier now.

### 10 of Wands

**Upright** - Overwhelmed, overworked, burned out, alcoholism, back problems, stress, can't handle any more responsibility, hiding from work, avoiding relationships and communication with others.

**Reversed** - Turn away from those who are not supportive of you, unload unnecessary responsibilities, free yourself from stress, drink more water and relax more, get help for addictions, take care of your health.

### Page of Wands

**Upright** - Messages through the mail, a young person who is creative, impulsive, on the go, sports oriented, physical, dynamic, learning about one's own power or sexuality, fun.

**Reversed** - Immature, not ready yet, no news coming, sexually immature or inexperienced, needs help channeling creative abilities or talents.

### Knight of Wands

**Upright** - A youth who likes adventure, physical, sexual, fun, likes pleasures, dynamic, aggressive, impulsive, travel and change, going forward but with some reserve, change of residence.

**Reversed** - Delays in moving forward or moving location, rash or impulsive behavior, angry personality or temperament, possible alcohol or physical abuse, need to slow down and examine things before acting or reacting.

### Queen of Wands

**Upright** - A woman who is creative, career minded, artistic, physical, sexual, aggressive or dynamic, outgoing, powerful, may use magic, likes nature, friendly, animal lover, possibly red-haired.

**Reversed** - Severe boss or administrator, makes rash decisions which may be unfair, misuse of power position, sexually frustrated or frustrated in general, rash temper.

### King of Wands

**Upright** - A man who is dynamic, friendly, sexual, sporty, creative, fun, outgoing, maybe a lawyer or in politics, could be a healer, writer, public speaker or teacher.

**Reversed** - May be possessive or angry at times, unfair treatment of others, cowardly or weak when he should be taking a stand, possible alcoholism or corruption in some way, needs to take a stand and speak up for himself.

**Wand people usually have red, auburn, reddish tinged or brown hair with blue or green eyes.**

**Their astrological signs most often are Aries, Leo and Sagittarius.**

# The CUPS

### Ace of Cups

**Upright** - Beginning of a new friendship or a new love opportunity, an invitation or offering, spiritual information coming, emotional replenishment, being offered some kind of help, new insights, divine protection, nourishment and sustenance.

**Reversed** - Unrequited love, opportunity does not come to pass, wasted energy, disillusioned.

### 2 of Cups

**Upright** - Partnership or love relationship, communication between two people, sharing, coming together, trust, compatibility, good foundation for a romantic relationship.

**Reversed** - Lack of communication, need for greater compromise and understanding, emotional immaturity, need for counseling.

### 3 of Cups

**Upright** - Celebration, social gathering such as a wedding or party, news of a birth, friends coming together, fun times, drinking.

**Reversed** - Overindulging in food and drink, falling out of friendship, things fruitful, but not as fruitful as one had hoped.

### 4 of Cups

**Upright** - Contemplation, boredom, emotional stagnation, not seeing the obvious or the gift being offered, possible inability to accept love, period of drying out, meditation, lack of clarity, unsure of oneself, focusing on the past.

**Reversed** - Beginning to see the gift being offered, taking attention off the past and looking at future possibilities, acceptance of where you are in the present, being able to finally move on, and appreciation for what one has been given.

### 5 of Cups

**Upright** - Emotional regret or sorrow, loss of some kind, mistakes made, in-between the past and the future, mourning, seeing the glass half empty instead of half-full, absorbed in ones shadow self, inability to see the positive, spending too much time in the past, self-pity.

**Reversed** - Shame, wanting to hide away from others, needing time to reconcile what has occurred with oneself and then others, needing to recover from emotional losses, stand back and see the bigger picture, need to begin to start again and rebuild. Watch health.

### 6 of Cups

**Upright** - Good friends, warmth, affection, past-life ties, trust, caring, comfort shared between friends, pure love, children or childhood friends, gift coming, possible engagement, protecting someone or being protected, innocence, sincerity, good karma.

**Reversed** - Look to the past or to someone from the past for help, comfort or guidance. Things are still good and there has been many gifts given and good accomplishments made. No need for worry. Possible transition time, but all will be well.

### 7 of Cups

**Upright** - Disillusionment, unable to ground desires into reality, fantasies, drug use or alcoholism, too many desires, lack of clarity, confusion, need to redirect the imagination.

**Reversed** - Seeing clearly after a period of confusion, ok to listen to counsel from others, strength regained, period of 'drying out', getting re-focused.

### 8 of Cups

**Upright** - Retreat or going on retreat, self-reflection, abandonment of current situation, searching for deeper understanding or meaning, need for greater intimacy, purpose, loneliness, a hermit.

**Reversed** - Self discovery, healing of old wounds, personal reconciliation and enlightenment, achieving greater understanding, compassion for others.

### 9 of Cups

**Upright** - The 'YES' card in the TAROT, happiness, fulfillment, satisfaction, culmination of desires, wish comes true, need to open heart more and be more sincere, overindulgence in food , drink, or drugs.

**Reversed** - Emotional satisfaction missing despite accomplishment, feeling of drudgery, disappointed in someone or something, feeling not understood, refusal to open up and share feelings or concerns.

### 10 of Cups

**Upright** - Happy home and love life, children, dreams come true, emotional success, close family; working together brings success, happiness and reward.

**Reversed** - More work to do, needs fulfilled but not perfect, need for music and singing, lonely for others despite having a happy family, need more personal self expression and diversity, plant a garden.

### Page of Cups

**Upright** - News via a phone call, birth announcement, a young person who is dreamy, imaginative, sensitive, emotional, psychic, likes water, possibly gay, communicative.

**Reversed** - Communication or phone call delayed, no news yet, patience needed, stay loving  and calm despite worry or fear, take a trip near water, keep your passion alive, have faith and trust, emotional immaturity.

### Knight of Cups

**Upright** - A youth who is flirty, romantic, sensitive, kind, loving, poetic, idealistic, an invitation, the hero or knight in shining armor, possibly fickle, love offering or engagement.

**Reversed** - Love interest moving away, sight is on another or another thing, emotional distraction, chasing dreams or fantasies, idealism, hopeless romantic who can never find perfection and therefore is not reliable or committed.

### Queen of Cups

**Upright** - A woman who is sensitive, kind, loving, romantic, idealistic, maternal, intuitive, psychic, deep, spiritual, nurturing, emotional, could be a psychic reader.

**Reversed** - Self effacing, too shy, gifted but too timid or weak to trust in yourself, needs not being met, needs emotional support and nourishment, very psychic but not speaking it, no one is listening.

### King of Cups

**Upright** - A man who is kind, sensitive, loving, romantic, likes water, intuitive, psychic, nurturing, emotional, sometimes unstable, generally good natured, needs to be able to relax and integrate his experiences and feelings.

**Reversed** - Needs some time out for self reflection, retreat near water, be careful near water, solo is best for awhile, wise counselor, deep feeling and kind, genuinely concerned for the welfare of others, may seem aloof.

**CUPS people usually have blonde hair and blue or green or green eyes.**

**Their astrological signs most often are Pisces, Cancer and Scorpio.**

# The SWORDS

### Ace of Swords

**Upright** - Onrush of swift and powerful energy, bringing clarity or courage or causing someone to act in a quick and decisive way for good or ill, cutting through, force, double-edged sword, use force wisely.

**Reversed** - Death to a person or situation, 'no' is the answer, inability to decide, conflict is ruining clarity of choice, put down the sword and call a truce, don't use force or aggression unwisely, peace is a two-edged sword, be graceful and gentle, but firm, time to give something or someone a rest.

### 2 of Swords

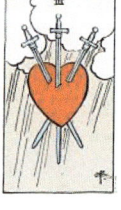

**Upright** - Caught between two choices, perceptions or opinions, unable to decide, temporary truce, stalemate, neutrality, having blinders on, poise, unsure of the outcome, other forces at work in the situation, pointing the finger at someone, not wanting to be involved.

**Reversed** - Staying balanced and firm in a difficult situation, holding 2 points of view of equal value, waiting for something to blow over, time will tell what will be decided, waiting patiently for the outcome.

### 3 of Swords

**Upright** - Heartbreak involving two or more people, love triangle, sorrow, loss, separation, breakup, abortion or miscarriage, grief, sometimes in the past rather than the present or future, the ending of a relationship, past, present or future, suffering from others affecting you, need to withdraw from a situation or from circumstance which does not involve you, need for self recovery.

**Reversed** - Let the past go, healing from emotional trauma or wounds, good health, having much love to give, heart operations successful, forgive others, bad weather for travel, beware of accident potentials, don't let other's drive your car.

Page | 37

### 4 of Swords

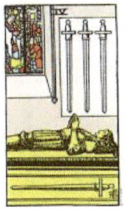

**Upright** - Retreat, rest from strife, recuperation, hospitalization, meditation, solace, needed healing, peace and tranquility, things on hold, timing not right for action, reviewing religious beliefs and doctrines.

**Reversed** - Prayers helping, lie low and concentrate, your inner self heals all your ills and troubles, you have your own power within, need a new bed, nurture and nourish yourself now, you have more strength than you think but need to take time for renewal, read and record your experiences.

### 5 of Swords

**Upright** - Arguments, power struggles, envy, jealousy, competition, blame, anger directed towards others or oneself, accusations, punishments, revengeful thinking or actions, strife, shame, defeat, going to war, victory in war, resentment, false pride, hidden enemies, gossip, humiliation.

**Reversed** - Damaging or hurting others by aggression and force, no conscience or remorse, conversely could mean someone who comes to the aid of another - picks up the pieces and repairs and helps heal wounds or trauma.

### 6 of Swords

**Upright** - Moving away from strife or difficulties, moving to a new location, period of positive movement, leaving the past behind, learning from experiences, positive move.

**Reversed** - Going backwards, unable to move, outer influences causing delay or return to old places or circumstances, feeling of temporary defeat, have to wait until things shift.

### 7 of Swords

**Upright** - Walking away from something before it is finished, sneakiness, cleverness, escapism or avoidance, getting out while the getting is good, stealth, lying or deceiving, cowardice, folly, gossip.

**Reversed** - Thievery, cheating, abandoning a bad situation, not giving notice, and letting others finish the job.

## 8 of Swords

**Upright** - Feeling held back, confined or trapped by past or current circumstances, imprisonment, being tied down, being held captive by one's own beliefs or fears or by the opinions of others, need to get out on one's own, possessiveness, soda-masochism, outside interferences.

**Reversed** - Freeing yourself from bondage, walking out or away from a bad or imprisoning situation, saying 'no' to abuse, standing up for oneself, time to take your power back, stop self-pity, decide to be strong, you can do it, stop listening to others who are negative or self-defeating, take blinders off and look ahead. Go forward - take the first steps. Just do it! Get the help you need.

## 9 of Swords

**Upright** - Despair, worry, depression, illness, loneliness, mental illness, suicidal tendencies, need for comfort, nightmares, hopelessness, pessimism, could be of one's own distorted thinking, insomnia, all of the above leaving one's life.

**Reversed** - Headaches, despair increased, eye or back problems, hormone imbalances, poor health, need to stop dwelling on the past or on current anxieties, get help, use protection techniques.

## 10 of Swords

**Upright** - Hitting bottom, psychic attacks, ruin, feeling defeated, death, accident, negative cycle that will soon pass, the worst is over.

**Reversed** - Loss of valuable energy or reserves, others can no longer hurt you, you will soon be renewed, take time to heal, surrender your losses and start over - misfortune could be the beginning of a new and better life.

## Page of Swords

**Upright** - Messages through thought or email, a young person who is astute, mental, observant, intelligent, aware, perceptive, witty, intellectual, analytical, ready to make a move or physically move, good with horses, eloquent speaker, fair-minded.

**Reversed** - Foolish or rash behavior, decide carefully, be patient and wait, gifted artist or poet, clairvoyant, good teacher.

### Knight of Swords

**Upright** - A youth who is aggressive, forceful, quick to act, compulsive, ready, courageous, sometimes acts without thinking, wants things in a hurry, impatient, progressive, and powerful.

**Reversed** - Need to take control of a situation, fight for what is right but be fair and just, use caution and then proceed, powerful leadership abilities, use influence wisely.

### Queen of Swords

**Upright** - A woman who is analytical, highly perceptive and intelligent, observant and fair-minded, compassionate, could be a widow or a woman separated or divorced, clear in insight and of a higher mind when positive, decisive, right, knowing, sees through others.

**Reversed** - Critical or domineering, quick to judge, unfair, opinionated but still highly intelligent, has a soft spot for those in need, expects others to do their best and won't settle for less, strong when challenged, has great endurance.

### King of Swords

**Upright** - A man who is more intellectual and opinionated rather than emotional or sensitive, could be a judge or someone in a position to decide matters, fair and highly reasonable in the positive, can be calm and easy, quiet and observant.

**Reversed** - Critical and cold in the negative, unfeeling, and judging with limited knowledge and foresight, weak internally, doesn't want the responsibility of leadership or decision-making, silent when he should be speaking up or acting.

**SWORD people are usually fair-haired, with any color eyes.**

**Their astrological signs most often are Gemini, Libra & Aquarius.**

# The PENTACLES

### Ace of Pentacles

 **Upright** - A new business opportunity or money-making proposition, an increase in self-awareness leading to an increased sense of well-being, start of a new abundant cycle, self-definition, rising above limitations into something more productive, being offered a gift of money.

**Reversed** - Obstacles to achieving the money you need or desire, being held back by others, self-esteem needs to be boosted, may not be feeling well, misuse of money which is causing lack, repressed energies.

### 2 of Pentacles

**Upright** - Financial instability, two or more jobs at once, indecision about financial or work matters, in-between jobs, imbalance or fluctuation in emotions due to financial instability, roller-coaster, being at opposite ends with someone or something, things up in the air.

**Reversed** - Considering the possibilities, making a decision about the best choice, clarity and strength returning allowing for positive action, may move to a new location, feeling capable once again and in control of one's life and circumstances.

### 3 of Pentacles

**Upright** - A new project coming together or finishing the initial stages of a project, apprenticeship, submitting plans for approval, artistry, some expertise gained in some area but there is more to learn, arts and crafts, flea markets or craft fairs, the coming together of a project, work being accepted, take constructive criticism as a positive thing.

**Reversed** - Delays on the finishing of a project but all will turn out well, take the advice of others who are more experienced, be patient, spiritual guidance will come, keep records and plans on paper, more education may be needed.

### 4 of Pentacles

**Upright** - Security gained, status quo, can be a hoarder, limitations in going further, fear to move out of current comfort zone, insecurity on a personal level, inhibited, fear of success, grounded or not grounded, inability to let go, self defamation, treading on thin ice, rigid behaviors or viewpoints.

**Reversed** - Throwing caution to the wind, health returning, letting go of a stagnant lifestyle or way of doing things, having the confidence to go further, going back to school or taking a new job or position, may move to a new location, letting go of old fears and restrictions, opening up to new ideas and possibilities.

### 5 of Pentacles

**Upright** - Unemployment or job loss, financial hardship or instability, changes in finances, need to reevaluate current lifestyle or conditions, illness possible, seeking guidance, wanting to succeed but having a hard time, needing change, need to bring spirituality back into your life, prepare for cold climate.

**Reversed** - Spirituality regained, things getting better and moving forward, release of victim consciousness, making a decision for wellness, bring children into your life or do something to help others, to give is to receive.

### 6 of Pentacles

**Upright** - Promotions or loans granted, help financially or giving help to someone, generosity, benefactors, gifts, financial balance, gain, rewards, winning something, receiving what is due to you, paying off debts, gratitude is the key to prosperity, balance giving with receiving.

**Reversed** - Money given but not enough, not feeling deserving, have been put down by others, homeless person or situation, do what you can to find work, any amount of pay will increase your self-esteem, bank loan denied or for a lesser amount than needed, don't lose confidence - you can get back on your feet.

## 7 of Pentacles

**Upright** - Material accomplishments, resting period after earned successes or hard work, evaluation before proceeding further, gardening, fruition, vacation, strength and maturity gained, a level of satisfaction and peace achieved.

**Reversed** - Not satisfied with progress to date, re-evaluating a situation or outcome, a perfectionist who wants to do better, a good crop this year, fertilize soil for fruits and vegetables, working with the earth or environment is a good choice, natural healer - use your talents and abilities to achieve greater success, gifted with your hands.

## 8 of Pentacles

**Upright** - Laborer, executive or craftsman, expertise, workaholic, material gain through hard work and attention to detail and skill, conservative, physically strong, endurance, practicality, natural medicine, something you have been steadily building on is coming to fruition.

**Reversed** - Fatigue from overwork, need time off, you can relax now - success has been achieved, pass on skills and expertise to others, building a new house, making plans for retirement, good things ahead.

## 9 of Pentacles

**Upright** - Material wealth, independence, luxury, comfort, stability, accomplishing something by one's own efforts or success through a benefactor, being a benefactor, not for profit organizations or charities, well-being, strong inner guidance and protection, medicines from herbs that heal.

**Reversed** - Lonely, need other's in your life, wisdom achieved to share, prosperity and well-being, take time to listen to others, be more generous, isolation is not good for you.

### 10 of Pentacles

**Upright** - Inheritance, family owned business, wealth, good family, group living together, money coming in soon, sometimes unexpected, investing in multi-family homes or commercial projects, building a health center or spiritual retreat, projects involving nature, animals or children all good, community service or donating to hospitals, lucrative investing.

**Reversed** - Family disagreements around money or inheritance, settlement of estates, watch projects and investments carefully, written legacies, make sure everything is in writing and legally prepared, old ruins, preserving a dynasty or letting it fall away, stay grounded and plan wisely, holistic medicine will heal you or someone close to you.

### Page of Pentacles

**Upright** - Messages through the mail, a young person who likes and needs security, loves animals and nature, even-tempered, good-natured, industrious, schooling, need for more education, could work with the earth or environment, planning for a family.

**Reversed** - Moving too slowly to achieve desired result, need more motivation or self-confidence, believe in yourself, young person who could be a doctor or healer, eat more grains and greens, strong physical constitution, allowing jealousy of others to stifle your own growth, watch driving.

### Knight of Pentacles

**Upright** - A slow moving person but methodical, security-minded, likes nature and animals, reliable, offers a simple but secure life, practical, grounded, earthy, likes hiking and camping, generous and hard working, may need to open up more and share his or her feelings, watch stomach and intestines.

**Reversed** - Avoiding the help and guidance of others, wanting to go it alone, retreat, taking a new path towards personal growth, prosperity, or education, could be a vet, holistic practitioner or work with the environment, loves animals, the earth and the elderly. Quiet, but deep-feeling, knowledgeable and observant. Eat only organic foods.

### Queen of Pentacles

**Upright** - A woman who is wealthy and practical, who likes her home, gardens, nature and herbs, a good business woman, luxury-minded, physical, healthy, abundant and nurturing, strong, likes horses and animals, generous to those she loves, well respected and wise, may own her own business.

**Reversed** - Sadness from loss of family , wealth or inheritance, lonely, needs friendships to help, beautiful gardener, close to nature, highly sensitive, needs exercise for health, take a vacation near water or at a mountain spa, write books, cookbooks or keep a journal.

### King of Pentacles

**Upright** - A man who is wealthy and practical, excellent in business, may be the head of a company, kind and generous, stable, likes to accomplish on the material plane, builder, may be closed-minded to alternative ways of doing things, materialistic, has many possessions, investor, stocks, loves taking care of family, strong protector.

**Reversed** - Selfish with money and wealth, insensitive boss or patriarch, doesn't listen well to others, stubborn, set in ways, uses power to control others or situations, watch feet and circulation in legs, needs to be near water for balance and sensitivity, hearing could be affected, likes horses and rides well, may have a boat or yacht, physically attractive and powerful.

**Pentacle people are usually dark or white-haired. May be dark skinned with dark or gray eyes.**

**Their astrological signs most often are Capricorn, Taurus and Virgo.**

# NUMBER VALUES

## ONES

… mean new beginnings, initial stages, not yet in form, individual, unique, independent, singular.

## TWOS

… are pairs, dualities, options, choices, decisions, partnerships, unions, opposites.

## THREES

… are groups, culminations, progress, results, expression.

## FOURS

… mean stability, set, limited, finite, ordered, fixed, structured.

## FIVES

… are changes, instability, in-between, chaotic, movement, middle, creative.

## SIXES

… mean harmony, success, accomplishment, communication, progress, family.

## SEVENS

… are victories, accomplishments, new awareness, spirituality, higher understanding.

## EIGHTS

… mean maturity, goals realized, material success, power both personal and in the world.

## NINES

… are culminations, peaks, accomplishments, concentration, endings.

## TENS

… are outcomes, finishes and new beginnings, arriving, fullness, completion.

# TAROT CARD SPREADS

## Important Notes on Spreads

In doing **TAROT** spreads, it is important to pay attention to the querent's **QUESTION**. A spread is like steps, beginning with card #1, going on to card#2, gathering information through each card and its position and then building a story as it goes along.

Each card's **POSITION** tells you what to focus on when interpreting the meaning of a particular card. Each card in the reading will give its own piece of information and will give you a good picture of where the client is heading in the final outcome.

Remember that a **TAROT** spread is not an absolute - many situations and outcomes can be changed by bringing aspects to conscious awareness allowing for different decisions to be made which can change entire outcomes.

Don't worry if you can't get it right away - with the **TAROT** practice makes perfect!

Many people get hung up on seeing **REVERSED** cards. As I mentioned in the Frequently Asked Questions (FAQs) section, you always have a choice when using the **TAROT** and doing a spread to pull the cards either solely **UPRIGHT** or **UPRIGHT** & **REVERSED**. Many users of the **TAROT** like to let the cards fall as they may while other users prefer to turn all the cards **UPRIGHT**.

I have personally done it both ways, but now I pull them all upright. There is no right way or wrong way to do it.

I have provided in this book both upright and reversed aspects of each card, giving you the option to intuit meanings from both. What I do suggest, however, is to decide ahead of time which way you are going to lay your spread out. This will give the message to your subconscious mind and will assure you of an accurate answer to your query or focus.

# SIMPLE 3-CARD SPREAD

## Card No. 1 - The Past

This card represents what has occurred in the past regarding the client's question/situation or what the energy has been around it in the past. The past could be what happened yesterday or it could have been a few days, months or years ago. It isn't important to know the exact time - it is only important to know that this card represents a past occurrence or influence.

## Card No. 2 - The Present

This card represents what is going on in the present regarding the client's question/situation or what the energy is at present.

## Card No. 3 - The Future

This card represents where the situation or question is heading based upon the information in the first two cards. It shows what the future result will most likely be if the client makes no changes or new decisions.

### Example 3-Card Spread Reading

*Querent question: Am I going in the right direction with my work?*

The Past    The Present    The Future

### Card 1 - 7 of Wands - The Past

In this card we see a young man holding a wand in a position of strength. He looks to be in control of a challenging situation. He is holding his ground, although he is tired of the struggle.

**Interpretation, considering the question...**

Page | 48

In the past (could be recent or long standing) the querent has held his position in his career or job, although it hasn't been without hard work, challenges and long hours. He is tired of this now, and desires some relief.

### Card 2 - Queen of Swords - The Present

**Card 2** shows a woman of the Sword suit. This tells us that she is direct, possibly in a position of power such as a boss or manager, and is decisive and quick thinking.

**Interpretation, considering the question...**

This woman could be the querent's boss or the querent themselves. It tells us a decision is about to be made regarding the querent's career or job position. Clear thinking and action is required.

### Card 3 - 9 of Cups - The Future

This card shows 9 upright cups in bright yellow. The background is also bright yellow and there are blue curtains. A happy man is sitting proudly in front of the cups.

**Interpretation, considering the question...**

The 9 of Cups is the **'YES'** card in the **TAROT**. It tells us the answer is **'yes'** to the querent's question or is positive. The querent can look forward to better times ahead.

### Putting it all together...

This simple 3-card spread tells us the querent has worked hard in his/her job but is a bit weary of the challenges. Still, they are in a strong position within the company. The querent may decide to make a job change and if so, should make the decision with a clear mind and confidence. If they do not get a new job, their current job will be reviewed by their boss who will make a decision about it. Either way, the querent can look forward to better and happier times.

# THE TRADITIONAL CELTIC CROSS SPREAD

## Card No. 1 - The Current Situation

**Card 1** shows what is going on presently in a situation or query. It will usually simply show the question or focus of the reading - in other words, it will reflect the question being asked.

## Card No. 2 - The Crossing Influences for Positive or Negative

**Card 2** shows what is 'crossing' or influencing the situation or query for positive or negative. The card pulled will reflect this. If it is a positive card, it shows positive influences towards the querent or situation. If it is a negative card, it can show sabotaging influences toward the client or situation from the client themselves or from outside influences.

## Card No. 3 - The Foundation of the Issue

**Card 3** shows the underlying energy of the situation or what is really going on beneath the surface of the situation or question. This position can be very interesting because it may show energy or influences beneath the surface that were not known or expected by the querent. These can be from others or from the clients own emotional, mental, physical or spiritual self. This card is the springboard for the events occurring in the situation or question.

## Card No. 4 - The Recent Past

**Card 4** tells us what has just occurred recently in regards to the query or what the past energy affecting the querent has been. It could have been days, weeks, months or years ago but whichever it is, it is still influencing the querent or situation today. It can also indicate an energy or influence that is no more applicable in the querents life.

## Card No. 5 - The Near Future

**Card 5** shows us where the querent is heading at this time in regards to the situation or query. This card will show how the querents future is being molded based upon the information in the previous cards.

Page | 50

### Card No. 6 - The Further Future

**Card 6** tells us what is likely to come into being based upon what is happening or has happened so far in the situation or query. Since Card 5 and Card 6 are future cards, they have not yet come into being but are heading in a certain direction. If your querent likes this direction, good - if they do not, then discussions are appropriate as to what changes could be made to avoid an unwelcome future.

### Card No. 7 - The Clients Attitude in the Situation

**Card 7** reveals how the client feels or is thinking about the query/situation. It DOES NOT show what has happened - only what the client is thinking or feeling. This card too can invite conversation or guidance around feelings or attitudes that could need changing for a more positive result to occur.

### Card No. 8 - Outside Influences or Environment

**Card 8** reveals to us the influence of outside factors affecting the situation - such as other people involved, cosmic forces, timing etc. It gives the querent a heads up on influences they may have not have been aware of for good or ill.

### Card No. 9 - Hopes and Fears

**Card 9** tells us the predominant energy of the client in terms of their expectations in the query - if the card is positive it is the best they hope for and if it is negative it is their worst expectation. Neither expectation may be actualities, however.

### Card No. 10 - The Final Outcome based upon the Previous Cards

**Card 10** tells the probable outcome of the situation based upon all the other cards. Remember that many situations can be changed with a change in the individuals involved, if so desired. If your querent is happy with all the cards and the outcome, no changes need to be made.


### An example Reading of the Celtic Cross Spread follows on the next page...

Page | 51

### Example Celtic Cross Spread Reading

*Querent's question - Should I consider moving and if so, will I be able to find work easily in the new location?*

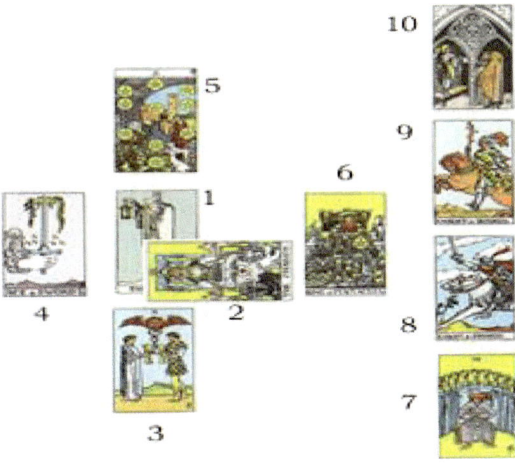

### Card 1 - The Hermit - The Present Situation

The Hermit is a card of spiritual guidance, enlightenment and self-reflection. Because it is in the **'present'** position, it indicates that the querent is being guided and his/her thoughts of moving may be coming from his/her Inner Guidance.

### Card 2 - The Chariot - What's Crossing for Good or Ill

The Chariot is a card of travel and movement. In this position it would indicate a strong support for moving. Because it is a **MAJOR** card, it is showing that this is a move that is good for the querents spiritual or soul progress.

### Card 3 - 2 of Cups - The Foundation of the Issue

The **2 of Cups** is a good communication card showing harmony in relationships. In relation to the question, it shows the move will be good for relationships and to include your partner every step of the way. If there is no partner, it shows good relationships developing as a result of the move.

### Card 4 - Ace of Swords - The Recent Past

The **Ace of Swords** in this position indicates a rush of clarity and energy. It supports new ventures, choices, and actions. 'Now is the time'.

Page | 52

### Card 5 - 10 of Pentacles - The Near Future

The **10 of Pentacles** is a wonderful family, prosperity and tradition card. In relation to the question, it shows good karma from the past along with financial support. It can also be encouraging going into business for yourself.

### Card 6 - King of Pentacles - The Further Future

The **King of Pentacles** describes a man with dark features - skin, hair, eyes - who is wealthy and a good provider. He may own his own business or be the head of a corporation, for example. In relation to the question, he may indicate a new boss for the querent or, if the querent should go into his own business, he would do very well. Either way, it is showing that he will do well financially with his intended move and work.

### Card 7 - 9 of Cups - The Querent's Attitude in the Situation

The **9 of Cups** is the **'YES'** card in the **TAROT**. It shows happiness and fulfillment. In relation to the question, it is showing the querent's attitude is one of positive expectation and happiness about moving.

### Card 8 - Knight of Swords - Outside Influences

The **Knight of Swords** describes a young man who is quick to act, is determined, and sometimes make rash decisions. He is fair in skin, hair, and eyes. Considering the question and the position this card holds, the **Knight** indicates that it is a good time to be moving, that the universal energy is supportive of it and to make the decision for it. Because it is a Sword card, it may also indicate the timing for the move - in this case the Autumn.

### Card 9 - Knight of Wands - Querent's Hopes or Fears

The **Knight of Wands** describes a young man who is proceeding forward on his steed with fiery energy. He is positive, aggressive, and takes action. In relation to the question and the position of the card - (hopes and fears) - it is showing the querent is ready to go, that he/she has the energy for the move. The querent may be HOPING to go in the Summer (since the **Knight** is of the **Wand** suit), but he/she may not actually go until the Autumn, as indicated by the previous card (**Knight of Swords**).

**Note:** If the card in this position had not been positive, you would have read it as a FEAR of the querent as opposed to a HOPE if the card is positive. In either case, this position is only showing the querent's hopes or fears and NOT what is actually occurring in the situation.

### Card 10 - 3 of Pentacles - The Final Outcome

The 3 of Pentacles is a card of initial projects coming to fruition, of cooperation among those involved, of planning and preparing. In relation to the question, the **3 of Pentacles** is showing the need for careful planning and preparing to ensure the upcoming move goes smoothly and successfully. It encourages good work prospects and teamwork.

### Putting it all together...

This reading is a very strong support for moving forward and tells that the move and work prospects the querent is asking about is a positive change ensuring new growth, the possibility for new business - self generated or otherwise. Although the querent would like to move immediately, the reading is suggesting to plan and prepare for the move, even if it means waiting until the Autumn.

# THE MANIFESTATION SPREAD

This spread can be used either for a desire of your own that you would like manifested or for a client.

## Card No. 1 - The Desire to be Manifested (the SEED card)

For **Card 1**, have the querent go through the Tarot deck and pick the card that they feel represents their desire to be manifested and place it in Position 1. This is the ONLY card in the spread that is picked by the client deliberately. For the rest of the spread, shuffle the cards and pick randomly as you normally would.

## Card No. 2 - The Emotional Adjustment Needed

**Card 2** represents a shift that needs to occur in the querent's emotional feelings about the desire to be manifested. If the card is positive, no shifts needs to be made – if it is negative, discuss emotional changes that need to be made with your client to support their desired manifestation.

## Card No. 3 - The Mental Adjustment Needed

**Card 3** represents a mental shift that needs to occur in the querent's attitude, opinions or perception for the manifestation to occur. If the card is positive, no shifts need to be made - if it is negative discuss mental changes that need to be made with your client to support their desired manifestation.

## Card No. 4 - What of the Past to Leave Behind

**Card 4** tells the querent what in their past they need to release or leave behind for their desire to manifest. This could be a location/place, people, relationships, attitudes, emotional blockages etc. The card pulled will reveal which it is.

## Card No. 5 - What of the Future to Allow

**Card 5** shows the querent what they need to allow to happen with regards to the desired manifestation. This card will show an area where the querent needs to allow for things to happen. If the card is positive, no shifts need to be made - if it is negative discuss changes that need to be made with your client to support their desired manifestation.

### Card No. 6 - What to Be Willing to Give Out

**Card 6** tells the querent what effort or action they need to take to support the manifestation of their desire. This card can be a great help in showing actions to take to make the desire come into reality.

### Card No. 7 - What to Be Willing to Receive

**Card 7** shows what the querent needs to be willing to receive in order for the manifestation to occur. Receiving can be an issue for some people – especially if they are not use to getting what they want. The card in this position will show you if the client can receive easily or needs to learn to receive. Either way, being able to receive is an important factor for any manifestation to occur.

### Card No. 8 - What is needed to Fertilize the Seed Card (Card 1 is the 'seed' card)

**Card 8** tells the querent the energetic requirement needed - the extra energy - it could be on any level - physical, emotional, mental or spiritual that is needed for the manifestation to occur. As things always begin in the energy field first, what the card in this position shows can determine the success or failure of the desired manifestation.

### Card No. 9 - What to Put Into the Auric Field

**Card 9** is a visualization card. It will represent an energy, idea or emotion to visualize being filled into the querent's auric field to build up the magnetic/attractive energy for the manifestation to occur. The Law of the Universe is 'Like Attracts Like'. The querent must have an auric or magnetic energy that is similar in quality or frequency to the desire they want to manifest. If the card is positive, no shifts needs to be made – if it is negative, discuss changes that need to be made with your client to support their desired manifestation and what the new visualization should look like.

### Card No. 10 - The Gift from Your Higher Self

**Card 10** is a blessing card from your Higher Self to help support the manifestation of your desire. If you pull a card in this position that appears negative, it may be suggesting that your desire isn't based on your highest good and that you should reconsider it. It could also be giving the client information they need to know about the manifestation and the card revealed will show this. If it is positive, it is a **'go ahead'** card - you have the support of your Higher Self in the manifestation.

## Example Manifesting Spread Reading

*Querent's Desire to Be Manifested – Wealth and a New Home*

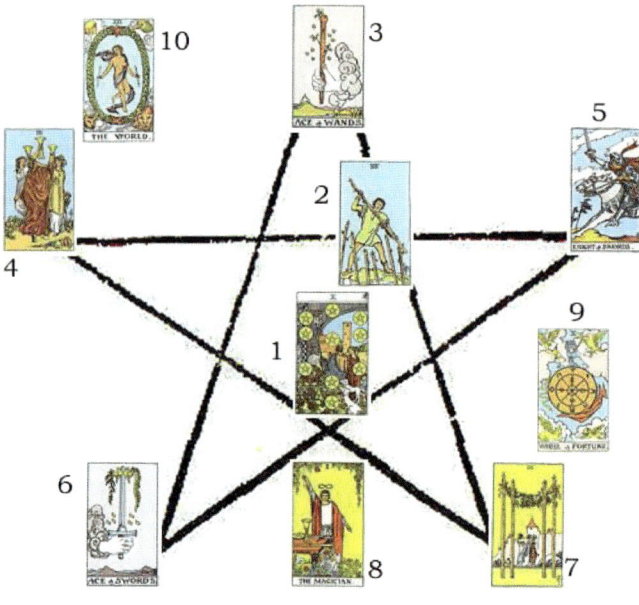

## Card 1 - The SEED Card

The client has gone through the deck and picked the card that to them reflects their desire. In this case it is the 10 of Pentacles – a card of wealth, home and financial success.

## Card 2 - 7 of Wands - the EMOTIONAL Shift Needed for the Manifestation to Occur

The **7 of Wands** shows a person maintaining a position of strength and perseverance and overcoming challenges. Because this card is in the emotional position, it tells the client that he/she must be emotionally determined, strong and persevering for their goal to manifest. They need to maintain a positive stance and overcome challenges as they come along without feeling overwhelmed or defeated by them. Keep going despite obstacles or challenges.

Page | 57

### Card 3 - the Ace of Wands - the MENTAL shift Needed for the Desire to Manifest

The **Ace of Wands** is an onrush of creative and inspirational energy. It is a NEW energy (being an **Ace** or **1**). Because this card is in the mental position, it shows the client that they must be open to new ideas, attitudes and new creative ways of doing things to succeed. Explore new ways from yourself or others before proceeding.

### Card 4 - 3 of Cups - What of the PAST to Leave Behind

The **3 of Cups** is a card of celebration, social occasions, friends and partying. In this position – what of the past to leave behind, it indicates that it is time now to get down to business after much socializing. It can also indicate that the client's new manifestation of wealth and a new home may be taking them out of a familiar area where friends and family exist.

### Card 5 - The Knight of Swords - What of the FUTURE to Allow

The **Knight of Swords** is a card of swift moving action, decisiveness, strength and courage. In this position - what of the future to allow - it is suggesting to allow for a fast and quick change. It offers courage and strength for personal support. It encourages taking the risk.

### Card 6- Ace of Swords - What to Be Willing to GIVE OUT

The **Ace of Swords** is a card offering an onrush of mental clarity, power for action and swift decisions. In this position - what to be willing to give out - it is suggestion that a decision needs to be made and if it is, new ideas and clarity of thought will follow. In other words, you will know what to do to implement or take action on your plans. The strength and courage to do so will be there to support you.

### Card 7 - The 4 of Wands - What to Be Willing to RECEIVE

The **4 of Wands** is a card of co-operation, harmony and success in business and personal affairs. In this position - what to be willing to receive - this card indicates that the client must be willing to allow for success and harmony to come into his/her life. This sounds easy, but if a person is used to struggling, allowing success and harmony to be his/her new reality can be something to receive and integrate into one's consciousness.

### Card 8 - the Magician - What is Needed to FERTILIZE the Seed Card

The **Magician** is a **Major Arcana** card representing the conscious mind and the power of **'as above, so below'**. It tells how we create our realities by what we think, believe and perceive. It is also a card of focused attention, concentration and action. In this position - what is needed to fertilize the seed card - it is letting the client know that he/she needs to stay focused, visualize and take action to achieve their goal.

### Card 9 - Wheel of Fortune - What to Put Into the Auric Field

The **Wheel of Fortune** is another **Major Arcana** card indicating cycles of change and new fortune. In this position - what to put into the auric field - it is telling the client to energize their manifestation by visualizing their lives taking a positive shift towards good fortune and positive movement towards success. This card will help provide positive movement and will help build up a strong magnetic energy in the client's auric field which will allow them to attract their good into their lives.

### Card 10 - The World - the GIFT from the Higher Self

In this Major Arcana card, the gift of satisfaction and personal fulfillment is being offered. The World indicates a return to wholeness. In this position - the gift from the Higher Self - the client is assured the success of his/her manifestation and is being shown that his/her Higher Self supports the manifestation.

### Putting it all together...

This reading encourages the client's desires for a new home and wealth. It is saying the desire is a good one and will provide positive movement and growth. The client is to stay focused, take action, make firm decisions and allow change to occur. The timing is right and the energy needed to materialize this desire is now available.

# THE PHYSICAL HEALTH SPREAD

In examining the cards in this spread, use your intuition to provide the information required. If you feel you need to develop your intuition, you can use the **Intuitive Exercise Using Color, Number & Symbol** on the following pages as a way to intuit the messages from the cards. You can also use the **meanings of the cards and numbers** in the beginning of this book to seek a word or phrase that may provide the answers you seek.

In reading spreads like this, it is important to remember the focus of the spread - physical health - and the positions of the cards in the light of your question. This is explained in detail as we go through the example spread.

CAUTION PLEASE - YOU ARE NEVER TO TELL ANYONE THEY ARE DYING OR THAT YOU SEE DEATH FOR THEM IN THE CARDS!

Many conditions can be changed and you must always look for a positive shift for your client whenever possible.

|   1   |   2   |   3   |   4   |   5   |

## Card No. 1 - The Current Condition of the Body

**Card 1** gives you an **OVERALL VIEW** of your client's physical condition. To use your intuition, allow yourself to get an immediate feeling or impression at first glance and make a note of it on your paper. You might feel positive and light in which case you would interpret that to mean your client is generally in good health. Conversely you may feel worried or disturbed when you look at the card in which case you would know something is amiss even if you can't get what it is specifically yet.

Page | 60

### Card No. 2 - The Specific Area of Concern

**Card 2** helps you focus on a **SPECIFIC AREA** of the body needing attention. Let yourself scan the card as if it were superimposed over the body and notice if you keep stopping at a part of the card that would be over a certain area of the body. You may also notice a dark area on the card that your attention keeps going to. You might also just have a knowing or feeling as you look at the card. Whatever you intuit, make a note of it on your paper.

### Card No. 3 - Cause of Current Condition

**Card 3** helps reveal the underlying **CAUSE** of the condition or imbalance. With this card, you will look at the card and ask it to help you see what the cause of the condition is for your client. It could be emotional, mental, physical or spiritual. It is important to learn to relax and let the card 'talk' to you to intuit this information. Don't be concerned if you don't get it right away - or - if you DO get it right away don't censor your intuition!

### Card No. 4 - Changes to Make to Heal the Body

**Card 4** points to **CHANGES** that need to be made to correct the imbalance. It could be diet, exercise, rest, seeing a doctor, surgery, energy therapy or any number of possibilities. Once again, ask the card to tell you. Make a note of it.

### Card No. 5 - Visualization Card to Further Healing

**Card 5** is a **VISUALIZATION** card to use to further assist in the healing process. If the card pulled in this position is positive, have your client visualize the image daily. If the card appears to be negative, find out what its message is for the client and have them focus on affirming a new thought or belief about themselves. If your client does not have a TAROT deck themselves to use as a visualization focus, discuss with them the positive meaning of the card pulled here and have them affirm these qualities daily.

## Example Physical Health Spread Reading

*Querent's Question – How is my health or my physical condition?*

1         2         3         4         5

### Card 1 - The Tower - Overall Condition of the Body

The **Tower** is a card of disruption from within. It indicates things are in need of change or are in a state of disruption. In this position - overall condition of the body - it would indicate that the body is breaking down or in need of major change to ensure health.

### Card 2 - The Hanged Man - Specific Area of Concern

The **Hanged Man** is a card of reversing perception, relaxation or inaction. Seen from a negative stance it can indicate a victim or martyr complex. In this position - the specific area of concern - it indicates that the client needs some rest and relaxation, that their attitudes or perceptions may need changing (they may be seeing themselves as a victim). In this case, they may be bringing on their own illness by refusing to change or stubbornly adhering to old patterns or routines.

### Card 3 - The 10 of Wands - The Cause of the Current Condition

The **10 of Wands** shows a person carrying a heavy load. He/she is overburdened or overwhelmed and could have back troubles. In this position - the cause of the physical condition - this card shows the client needing to take time off or lighten their load in some way. They are taking on too much at one time. They may also be taking on responsibilities that belong to others and need to let them go. The card is saying that if the client does not slow down they will be jeopardizing their health further and that their body is letting them know it is weakening or suffering under the strain. Another phrase for this card is 'Burn out'.

Page | 62

### Card 4 - The Page of Cups - Changes to Make to Heal the Body

The **Page of Cups** is a card of good news coming or of an opportunity being presented that is coming from a loving source. It can be the clients own inner guidance giving them a message showing love and concern for the client. In this position - changes to be made to heal the body - the card is saying the client needs to love or take care of themselves more and that if they do so, the means to make it happen will also come. It is saying help is available and they should act on that help. They may need to take time off, review their load and make changes to lighten it. Assign some of the responsibilities they are taking on to others - it is overdue. The need for more fluids is also indicated.

### Card 5 - King of Swords - Visualization Card to Further Healing

The **King of Swords** represents a man who is strong, decisive, intelligent and clear thinking. He can also be a bit matter-of-fact and unemotional. He can be the querent or a doctor or person in a position to give good advice. In this position - visualization to further healing - this card advises the client to picture themselves strong, clear and determined to make the changes needed in their life. It can also be asking the client to affirm that the right help will also show up in their life.

## Putting it all together...

This reading points to a weakening or possible disruption in physical health due to the client overburdening themselves with responsibility and/or work. They may have a martyr complex which needs to change. The spread is saying they need to slow down and lighten their load or else their health will suffer more so. They could already have back problems or other health concerns. To avoid getting worse they must make some necessary changes NOW and take time for relaxation. It is a decision for the client to love themselves more and take better care of themselves through diet, exercise and a balance of work and pleasure. A good full-body massage would also help to start the process as well as a visit to a good holistic doctor or energy therapist.

# INTUITIVE EXERCISE WITH COLOR, NUMBER & SYMBOL

This exercise is designed to stimulate your intuitive abilities and to increase your powers of observation. You will **NOT** be relying on the meanings of the cards listed in the beginning of this book - instead, you will be focusing only on the (1) **COLOR**, (2) **NUMBER** and (3) **SYMBOL** on the chosen cards.

All of us have subconscious associations to colors, numbers and symbols. By tapping into your own subconscious associations you will be able to deem messages on the cards without looking up any written meaning. The more you practice this process, the stronger and clearer your intuitive feelings and perceptions will become. These abilities are invaluable when reading the TAROT for yourself or for a client.

## Here's how to do it...

Select one of the previously shown spreads for this exercise. Then, instead of looking up the meaning of the cards from the beginning of this book, ask yourself what **COLOR** stands out to you on the card. It need not be the most dominant color, indeed it could be a tiny spat of color somewhere on the card.  Make a note of it in your notebook.

Next, make a note of the **NUMBER** of the card.

Then note which SYMBOL stands out to you on the card. For example, is it a crown, a shoe, a garland, a staff or wand, a cup, a pentacle, a throne, the sea or sky etc? Whatever it is, make a note of it in your notebook.

Do this process for every card in the spread that you chose for this exercise. Then go back to **Card 1** in the spread and ask yourself what each of these three things mean to you - the **COLOR** you picked, the **NUMBER** and the **SYMBOL** you picked.

Try to **feel** their meaning in relation to the **question** you asked for the spread and the **position** of the card in the spread in relation to the question. Ask yourself; how did each of these make you **feel**? What did they make you **think** of? What **messages** do you think they are imparting to you?

Do this for each of the cards in the spread. Try to put this information together in a way that tells a story about what the reading may mean. Keep in mind the original query, and the meanings of the **POSITIONS** in the spread to help you in your interpretation. Practice summarizing the spread using this exercise. An example follows on the next page.

Page | 64

**COLOR**

**NUMBER**

**SYMBOL**

**Example using the Simple 3 Card Spread**

*Querent's Question - How can I increase my financial prosperity?*

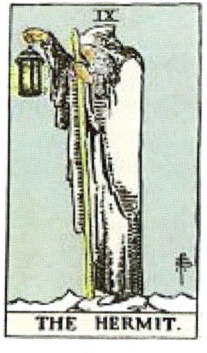  

**Card 1 Past**    **Card 2 Present**    **Card 3 Future**

## Card 1 - The Hermit - The Past

**COLOR** - Yellow    **NUMBER** - 9    **SYMBOL** -The Staff or Wand

The **COLOR Yellow** on this card AND IN RELATION TO THE QUESTION means to me: power, strength, illumination, inner guidance, reliance on spirit.

The **NUMBER 9** means to me: trials and tests, uphill climbing, feeling alone, attainment of my own, no outside help, inner progress.

The **SYMBOL** of the **Staff/Wand** means to me: inner support, wanting to lean on others, need guidance, need to rely on oneself, lack of self confidence, inability to trust, fatigue.

## Card 2 - The Ace of Swords - The Present

**COLOR** - Gray    **NUMBER** - Ace or 1    **SYMBOL** - The Sword

The color **Gray** in this card and considering the question, it means to me: despondency, inactivity, stalemate, being uninspired, no hope for change, bleakness, cloudy days.

The **NUMBER 1 (Ace)** means to me: start or begin again, rethink everything, take on a new challenge or make different decisions, this is about holding your own and regaining personal strength.

The **SYMBOL** of the **Sword** means to me:  push through obstacles and don't give up, have strength and courage, the choice is yours whether to succeed or fail, be clear and firm in what you want to achieve.

## Card 3 - The Empress - The Future

**COLOR** - Red    **NUMBER** - 3    **SYMBOL** - Her white gown

The **COLOR Red** means to me: love needs to be the basis for all your desires, love is the life-blood that propels all things into being; the foundation of the Universe is built upon love.

The **NUMBER 3** means to me: principles, cooperation, togetherness, pride, consideration of others, don't do it for yourself alone, be generous and loving, the three are really One, all things are connected.

The **SYMBOL** of the Empress's **white gown** means to me: faith and trust, love based upon purity of intention and desire, harmlessness, innocence and purity of thought and motive, being one with the cosmos and its forces, being in alignment with the powerful forces of creation because one's heart is pure, producing miracles from thought and intention alone, holding one's own in the Universe.

## Putting it all together...

With regard to the querent's question about increasing prosperity in his/her life, the spread is revealing that the querent has been going through trials and tests designed to increase a sense of inner guidance and inner support rather than relying on others or outer circumstances.

It is similar to dark nights of the soul where we are left to our own devices to overcome hardships or trials. We are put through an inner tempering process much like when a blacksmith is forging a sword to perfection.

We can see by the spread that the querent is tired and has become despondent with little hope of relief. He/she needs to maintain courage and strength.

The final card reveals that perhaps the intention of increasing prosperity does not have love as its foundation and this is why the results desired have not been forthcoming. The querent needs to be asking his/her inner self to restore the belief, faith and trust in love and be willing to open his/heart to others as part of the inter-connectedness of all things. Service to others needs to be the motivating force and emotion.

# MEDITATION WITH THE MAJOR ARCANA

For this exercise you will begin to get sensitive to the messages in the Major Arcana cards. You will be using them to reveal deeper aspects of yourself and to learn the virtues of the cards.

Begin this exercise by separating out the Major Arcana cards from the Minor Arcana cards in your TAROT deck. Place the Minors to the side as you will not need them for this exercise.

Next, make the intention to your Higher Self that you are going to pick a Major card that is the reflection of your state of consciousness at this time or represents a lesson you might need to learn.

Shuffle and randomly pull one Major from the deck. Put it upright if it is reversed. On the next page you can follow the example card I picked for this exercise.

Then examine the card using the **COLOR**, **NUMBER** and **SYMBOL** exercise. After you do this, try to summarize what you think the card is showing you about your state of consciousness at this time or a lesson you may need to learn.

Next, go to the **'MEANINGS OF THE CARDS'** section in the beginning of this book and look up the card you pulled. Read all the descriptions and see what jumps out at you. Make a note of it and do not censor a meaning even if you don't like it. Self-honesty is a pre-requisite to uncovering your natural intuitive abilities.

After you have done this and have concluded what you think the card is revealing to you, hold the card in your left hand and close your eyes. Sit quietly, calm your mind and try to FEEL the card.

**What kind of energies do you feel from it? Is it calming or disturbing? Do you enjoy feeling it or do you want to hurry and put it down? Does your body accept the vibrations of the card or does it resist it?**

Whatever it is you feel, allow yourself to continue to hold the card in your hand. Sit with it for at least 15 minutes. This will allow enough time for you to allow the energies of the card to shift until you arrive at a neutral or peaceful sense of completion. Pay attention over the next few days as to any changes that have occurred in yourself or your life in feeling, perceptions or body.

Page | 68

### Example Meditation with the Major Arcana

I shuffled the Major cards and I pulled **The World** card.

Using the **COLOR**, **NUMBER** & **SYMBOL** exercise:

The **COLOR** that stood out to me on this card was **Blue.** To me, this color means freedom, peace, the sky and the ocean, a breath of fresh air, Divine protection, and help when I need it.

The **NUMBER** of this card is **21**. To me, this number means accomplishment, seeing clearly, Truth, near the end of period of learning.

The **SYMBOL** that stands out to me is **her naked body**. To me, this symbol means the reconciliation of form, God-light in the body, being or feeling at one with all, the body is now balanced with spirit and both are appreciated for what they are. It also means freedom from despair, a new life and a new world.

### Putting it all together...

**The World** card as a state of consciousness, **MEANT TO ME** that I have achieved a certain level of peace and clarity. I am divinely protected and feel I am being looked after. It made me feel I may be moving closer to water and blue skies soon. I also felt better about my body and saw its value as part of Creation. I was no longer in despair about it and felt there was a type of 'ascension' going on within me. Part of my consciousness may have already moved to an alternate dimension.

Then, I looked through the meanings of **'The World'** in the beginning of this book. Key phrases that jumped out at me were: wholeness, completion, equilibrium, ascension of body or consciousness.

My interpretation of these for myself was that I have achieved a certain level of ascension in that my physical body feels as if it has become one with my spirit - I began understanding that they are the **same** - my body IS MADE from my spirit and is one with it. Because this is so, I am no longer in conflict or divided within - I am at peace with it. This awareness is a necessary piece in becoming whole for me.

After sitting silently and holding the card in my left hand, my body felt like it was made of water and light. It became one with my spirit and I felt I was in perfect peace and in perfect balance. **I AM THIS I AM**.

*Important: When doing the exercise of **COLOR**, **NUMBER** & **SYMBOL**, remember that the interpretations are **YOURS ALONE**. They are what **YOU** feel about the color, the number and the symbol you chose in relation to the focus of the card - in this case - your state of consciousness at this time or a lesson you may need to learn. What I have put here as an example is **MY** own associations with the color, number and symbol I chose for the card I pulled - **The World**. If you had pulled **The World** card for yourself in this exercise your meanings most likely would be very different from mine.*

**Notes:**

# About Aingeal Rose

**AINGEAL ROSE is available for private readings via phone by appointment from anywhere in the world. Email her from her World of Empowerment organization website at:**

## http://worldofempowerment.org

On that site, also see **AINGEAL ROSE'S** eBooks:

**Healing With the TAROT**
**Aingeal Rose's Book of Spreads**
**Indigo, Crystal & Rainbow Children**
**Twin Flames & Soul Mates**

**Tel: Ireland 087-6177925   USA 224-588-8026**

CPSIA information can be obtained
at www.ICGtesting.com
Printed in the USA
LVIC06n2023291113
3632291V00015B/167